Contents

Acknowledgments

This book has been compiled with the co-operation of the Foreign and Commonwealth Office and the Falkland Islands Government.

Cover Photograph Credit

COI Pictures

Britain and the Falkland Islands

London: H M S O

Researched and written by Reference Services, Central Office of Information.

ISBN 0 11 701757 4

HMSO publications are available from:

HMSO Publications Centre
(Mail, fax and telephone orders only)
PO Box 276, London SW8 5DT
Telephone orders 071-873 9090
General enquiries 071-873 0011
(queuing system in operation for both numbers)
Fax orders 071-873 8200

HMSO Bookshops
49 High Holborn, London WC1V 6HB   071-873 0011
Fax 071-873 8200 (counter service only)
258 Broad Street, Birmingham B1 2HE   021-643 3740   Fax 021-643 6510
Southey House, 33 Wine Street, Bristol BS1 2BQ   0272 264306
Fax 0272 294515
9-21 Princess Street, Manchester M60 8AS   061-834 7201   Fax 061-833 0634
16 Arthur Street, Belfast BT1 4GD   0232 238451   Fax 0232 235401
71 Lothian Road, Edinburgh EH3 9AZ   031-228 4181   Fax 031-229 2734

HMSO's Accredited Agents
(see Yellow Pages)

and through good booksellers

Introduction

The Falkland Islands have, with the exception of ten weeks of illegal Argentine occupation in 1982, been continuously, peacefully and effectively occupied by Britain[1] since 1833. Moreover, the Islanders have repeatedly expressed, through their democratically elected representatives, their desire to remain under British sovereignty.

The British Government has emphasised that it will not support any transfer of sovereignty against the wishes of the Falkland Islanders. It is committed to promoting the Islanders' political, social and economic development in a climate of peace and security under a government of their own choosing. In recent years, relations between Britain and Argentina have improved, both sides agreeing to discuss matters of mutual interest while maintaining their respective positions on sovereignty.

This book provides information about the history of the Falkland Islands, the current constitution, the economy, social welfare and the dispute with Argentina. It also covers South Georgia and the South Sandwich Islands, which are both British dependent territories claimed by Argentina.

[1]The term 'Britain' is used in this book to mean the United Kingdom of Great Britain and Northern Ireland; Great Britain comprises England, Wales and Scotland.

Geography and Population

Situated in the South Atlantic, the Falkland Islands archipelago lies about 772 km (480 miles) north-east of Cape Horn. It consists of about 200 islands, the largest being East Falkland and West Falkland. The total land area is some 12,173 sq km (4,700 sq miles). The archipelago is about 480 km (300 miles) from the nearest point on the South American mainland.

The coastline is deeply indented and there are many good anchorages. There are no inland waters apart from shallow lakes. The Islands are generally hilly except in Lafonia, the southern half of East Falkland. The highest points are Mount Usborne (705 m [2,312 ft]) on East Falkland and Mount Adam (700 m [2,297 ft]) on West Falkland.

Much of the upland is comparatively bare of vegetation and consists of eroded peat, scree and stone runs—'rivers' of angular quartzite boulders. Because of the climate there are no indigenous trees, the natural vegetation being grassland with some species of heath and dwarf shrubs. Bird and marine mammal life—geese, penguins, seabirds and seals—is diverse and relatively unspoiled. There are no native land mammals, although over the past 150 years rabbits, hares, foxes and others have been introduced and are well established. Legislation provides for the protection of most birds and certain mammals. Some islands are wildlife sanctuaries and reserves.

As for the climate, there is a narrow temperature range, strong winds, a fairly low rainfall evenly distributed throughout the year, and frequent cloud cover. At Stanley average monthly temperature varies between 9°C (49°F) in January/February and 2°C (36°F) in

July, although the wind chill factor makes the temperature seem colder. Snow has been recorded in every month of the year except February, but seldom lies for long. Average annual rainfall is about 609.3 mm (24 inches) and annual average sunshine 1,618 hours.

The People

The population is almost entirely of British origin. The first settlers, some of whose descendants still live on the Islands, began arriving in the first years after 1833 and the population increased to about 2,000 in 1900.

The 1991 census showed a population of 2,121 (excluding military and contract personnel), an increase of 205 since the previous census in 1986, thus reversing the decline experienced since it rose to a peak of nearly 2,400 in 1931.

The birth rate in 1990–91 was about 13 per 1,000 population and the death rate was 10 per 1,000.

Stanley is the only town and has a population of about 1,650. Elsewhere, the largest settlements are Goose Green and North Arm on East Falkland, and Port Howard and Fox Bay on West Falkland. English is the Islanders' language. There are Anglican, Roman Catholic and Nonconformist churches.

History

Navigators of several countries, including Captain John Davis in 1592 and Sir Richard Hawkins in 1594, have been credited with first sighting the Islands. However, of the various claims to priority of discovery, only that of the Dutch sailor Sebald van Weert in 1600 is conclusively authenticated.

The first known landing was in 1690 by Captain John Strong, who named the Islands after Viscount Falkland, then Treasurer of the Navy. French seal hunters, who were frequent visitors to the area in the eighteenth century, called the Islands 'Les Iles Malouines' after the seaport St Malo from which many of the French seafarers had sailed: hence the Spanish designation, las Islas Malvinas.

In 1764 a small French colony, Port Louis, was established in East Falkland. Three years later the settlement was handed over to Spain on payment of a sum then equal to about £24,000. The Spaniards renamed the settlement Puerto de la Soledad. Meanwhile a British captain, John Byron, had made a comprehensive survey of West Falkland in 1765 and noted the fine anchorage in Saunders Island, which he named Port Egmont.

The British Admiralty soon dispatched Byron's subordinate, Captain McBride, who arrived in Port Egmont in 1766 and established a British settlement of about 100 people there. When in 1770 a Spanish force compelled the British settlers to leave, Spain and Britain were brought to the verge of war. In 1771, after protracted negotiations, the Spaniards handed back Port Egmont to Britain, which re-established the settlement but withdrew it again in 1774 on grounds of economy. The British claim to sovereignty was, however, maintained and, as was then customary, a leaded plaque was left declaring the Falkland Islands to be 'sole right and property' of King George III.

The Spanish settlement on East Falkland was withdrawn in 1811, leaving the Islands uninhabited apart from visits by whalers and sealers from England and North America. In November 1820, Colonel Daniel Jowett, an American national, claimed formal possession of the Islands in the name of the Government of Buenos Aires. At the time, this Government, which had formally declared its independence from Spain in 1816, was not recognised by Britain or any other foreign power.[2] In the absence of diplomatic representation in Buenos Aires there is no reason to suppose that the British Government knew of Jowett's action, although a notice of it was subsequently published in *The Times* on 3 August 1821. No act of occupation followed Jowett's visit and the Islands remained without effective government.

There were subsequent attempts by private individuals, occasionally sponsored by the new Argentine Government, to settle the Islands between 1826 and 1833 but these were sporadic and ineffective. On 10 June 1829 the Argentine Government issued a decree setting out its rights which were allegedly derived from the Spanish Viceroyalty of La Plata. The Government said that 'circumstances had hitherto prevented this Republic from paying [the Falklands group] the attention ... which, from its importance, it demands', and purported to place under the command of a Political and Military Governor 'the Islands of the Malvinas and those adja-

[2]Britain recognised Argentina in 1825.

cent to Cape Horn in the Atlantic Ocean'. A second decree on the same date appointed Louis Vernet as Governor. Later Vernet said that the foundation of the colony was his own work, that he received no assistance from his Government and that the Islands paid no taxation. The British Government protested that the terms of the decree infringed British sovereignty over the Islands, which Britain had never relinquished. The Argentine Government formally acknowledged receipt of the protest but did not deny British sovereignty or send a reply.

In 1831 a United States warship, the *Lexington,* destroyed the fort at Puerto de la Soledad as a reprisal for the arrest of three American vessels by Vernet, who was attempting to establish control over sealing in the Islands. The *Lexington*'s commander, Captain Silas Duncan, declared the Falklands free of all government and they remained once again without visible authority until September 1832 when the Buenos Aires Government appointed Juan Mestivier as Governor on an interim basis. Mestivier sailed to the Islands at the end of 1832. Shortly after his arrival there was a mutiny among the soldiers and the newly appointed governor was murdered.

A British warship, HMS *Clio,* visited the area in January 1833. It was commanded by Captain Onslow, who had occupied Port Egmont on the uninhabited West Falkland a month earlier. During the January visit Captain Onslow found that the commander (Jose Pinedo) of a Buenos Aires schooner of war had placed the mutineers in irons and was attempting to restore order. Claiming the right of sovereignty over the Islands, Captain Onslow requested Commander Pinedo to leave. No force was used and Commander Pinedo departed, under protest, taking with him the majority of the settlers. British occupation of the Islands was then resumed under the control of a naval officer. In 1844 the seat of government was removed from Port Louis to Port William where the settlement was named Stanley.

In 1841 a civil Lieutenant-Governor was appointed and in 1843 the civil administration was put on a permanent footing by an act of the British Parliament. The Lieutenant-Governor's title was changed to Governor, and the first Executive and Legislative Councils were set up in 1845. Although there was a majority of official members in the Legislative Council until 1951, nominated unofficial members played an increasingly important part, and in 1949 members elected by universal adult suffrage were introduced into the Council.

The naturalist Charles Darwin, responsible for the theory of evolution, called at the Falklands in 1833 and 1834. He recorded the flora and fauna and his visits were commemorated in several place names; Darwin settlement, Beagle Ridge and Fitzroy settlement are named after the naturalist, his ship and the captain respectively.

The territory's early industry was exploitation, mainly for their hides, of wild cattle in East Falkland. In the 1870s a change-over from cattle to sheep took place, the former being killed off. A period of reasonable prosperity followed and in 1885 the territory became self-supporting.

Wireless communication with the outside world was opened in 1912, and in December 1914 the Islands were the scene of a British naval victory over the German admiral Graf von Spee who went down with his flagship.

During the second world war the Islands proved their value as a naval base. After their victory over the German Navy at the Battle of the River Plate in 1940, the British cruisers returned to Stanley to land the wounded, who were cared for in the local hospital for several weeks. Ten Spitfire aircraft were purchased with money voted by the Falklands Legislative Council in 1940. Over 150 Falklands people served in the British armed forces during the second world war.

The Dispute with Argentina

The Islands are the subject of a territorial claim by Argentina which says that it has succeeded to rights claimed by Spain in the eighteenth century.

Successive British Governments have had no doubts about British sovereignty over the Islands, which have been peacefully and effectively occupied by Britain since 1833, with the exception of ten weeks of illegal occupation by Argentina in 1982.

The Islanders are united in their wish to remain under British administration and sovereignty. In 1986 an independent poll of Island electors took place. Answered by 89 per cent, practically all respondents (94.5 per cent) said that they wanted to remain British. The British Government, therefore, maintains that in these circumstances the Argentine claim is contrary to the Islanders' right of self-determination.

British–Argentine Talks

In 1964 and 1965 the Islands' position as a non-self-governing territory was debated by the United Nations Committee of Twenty Four (on colonialism). In August 1964 the Islanders' elected representatives informed the Committee that the population wished to retain its association with Britain and not to become independent or associated with any other country. The British delegation to the

Committee therefore pointed out that the Argentine claim was contrary to the principle of self-determination recognised in Article 1 of the UN Charter. In December 1965 the UN General Assembly approved a resolution inviting Britain and Argentina to hold discussions with a view to finding a peaceful solution to the problem, bearing in mind the interests of the Islanders. In January 1966 the British and Argentine foreign ministers had talks in Buenos Aires, the joint communiqué stating that both had agreed that the discussion recommended by the General Assembly should be pursued through diplomatic channels.

While fully aware that the basic differences between Britain and Argentina over sovereignty remained, the British Government felt that a lasting *modus vivendi* between the Islands and Argentina had to be achieved through negotiations. At the same time it emphasised that such an arrangement had to be acceptable to the Islanders. In addition, Britain hoped that the negotiations would lead to some practical form of co-operation between the Islands and Argentina, considering that this would be in the Islanders' long-term interests.

In 1969 Argentina offered to discuss a lifting of its ban on direct communications between the mainland and the Islands. In 1970 special talks opened in London between British and Argentine delegations, the former including representatives of the Islanders. In 1971 agreements were reached covering air and sea communications, postal services, educational and medical facilities for Falkland Islanders in Buenos Aires, and customs measures. In 1974 an agreement was signed facilitating trade and the transport of goods between the Islands and the mainland. Another agreement allowed the Argentine state petroleum company to supply the

Islands with petroleum products. All these agreements lapsed with the 1982 Argentine invasion.

The findings of an economic survey of the Islands conducted in 1976 by Lord Shackleton underlined that the future development and diversification of the Islands' economy could only take place through closer co-operation with Argentina. In 1977 Britain, therefore, concluded that the time had come to consider whether a new framework of economic and political co-operation should be established with Argentina.

After detailed consultations with the Islanders and with the Argentine Government, terms of reference were agreed for British–Argentine negotiations on future political relations, including sovereignty, and on economic co-operation in the Islands and the south-west Atlantic in general. The terms of reference also stated that issues affecting the future of the Islands would be discussed and that negotiations would 'be directed to the working out of a peaceful solution to the existing dispute about sovereignty between the two states'. These negotiations would be 'without prejudice to the position of either government with regard to sovereignty over the Islands'.

Discussions between the two governments took place in New York in December 1977, where it was agreed to establish two parallel working groups on political relations, including sovereignty, and economic co-operation, to study these matters in depth. The working groups met for discussions in Lima in February 1978 and further talks took place at the end of this year and in March 1979.

A round of wide-ranging but exploratory talks was held with Argentina in April 1980. In these, Britain made clear that, although it remained convinced of British sovereignty, it was prepared to consider possible ways of achieving a solution acceptable to all the parties while being guided by the wishes of the Islanders.

In November 1980 Britain consulted the Islanders on possible bases for seeking a negotiated settlement, including freezing the dispute for a period so as to develop the Islands' resources or exchanging the title of sovereignty against a long lease of the Islands back to the British Government. At the same time Britain emphasised that any solution would have to preserve British administration, law and way of life for the Islanders and that any eventual settlement would have to be endorsed by the Islanders and the British Parliament.

In January 1981 the Falkland Islands Executive and Legislative Councils agreed that the British Government should hold further talks with Argentina in order to seek an agreement to freeze the dispute over sovereignty for a specified period of time.

Argentine Use of Force

In February 1981 talks were held with Argentina which made it plain that a freeze of the dispute was unacceptable. A year later another round of talks took place in New York, Britain's delegation including two Councillors from the Falkland Islands. Despite these discussions (see p. 33), Argentina invaded and occupied the Islands on 2 April, as well as two other British territories in the south-west Atlantic—South Georgia and the South Sandwich Islands.

In response to this use of force, Britain broke off diplomatic relations with Argentina, imposed an arms embargo on Argentina and introduced trade and financial restrictions. On 3 April the UN Security Council passed a resolution demanding an immediate withdrawal of Argentine forces and calling on Argentina and Britain to seek a diplomatic solution to their differences and to respect fully the principles of the UN Charter.

Diplomatic efforts to find a peaceful solution continued (see pp. 37–43) until May 1982 but foundered on Argentina's refusal to comply with the Security Council's resolution and its insistence that any solution had to provide for the transfer of sovereignty to Argentina.

Britain, therefore, decided to repossess the Islands by military force and the Argentine forces on the Islands surrendered on 14 June 1982.

Following the conflict Britain attempted to normalise its relations with Argentina. In September 1982 it agreed to the reciprocal lifting of financial restrictions imposed at the time of the conflict. The Argentine authorities failed to respond to a 1983 British proposal to restore the bilateral air services agreement.

Further Talks

After the restoration of democracy in Argentina, which was welcomed by the British Government, talks took place between the two governments in 1984. They were agreed on the basis that, if Argentina raised the question of sovereignty, Britain would refuse to discuss it and the discussion would then move on to practical issues of concern to both sides. The talks ended in deadlock because of Argentine insistence on linking discussion of practical issues with the issue of sovereignty over the Falkland Islands.

In a further bid to restore more normal relations, Britain lifted its ban on the import of Argentine goods in July 1985, but this was not fully reciprocated by Argentina.

The position changed with the election in May 1989 of Carlos Menem as President of Argentina. Soon after his inauguration Sr

Menem announced that Argentina wanted to improve relations with Britain and proposed bilateral talks at the United Nations. Both sides agreed to leave the issue of sovereignty over the Falklands to one side and a series of bilateral talks followed.

Meeting in Madrid in October 1989, both sides agreed to establish consular relations, to resume air and sea links and to hold discussions on fisheries and military confidence-building measures. In 1990 air and sea links between Britain and Argentina were resumed.

In February 1990 both sides agreed to re-establish diplomatic relations and to a military confidence-building measure, involving the reciprocal notification of all military movements and exercises in the south-west Atlantic. Changes were made to this system from October 1991: these have enhanced the Islands' security by giving Mount Pleasant Airport effective control over all air traffic over and around the Islands. It was also agreed that ships could approach to 15 nautical miles of the respective coastlines and that the required notice for military exercises would be reduced from 25 to 14 days.

Diplomatic relations were resumed on 26 February 1990 and the bilateral relationship has since developed further. There have been a number of ministerial and official visits and agreements signed on the abolition of visas, cultural co-operation, investment promotion, air services and measures against drug trafficking. A visit by Argentine relatives to the Argentine cemetery on the Falkland Islands took place in March 1991.

Following another meeting in Madrid in November 1990, the South Atlantic Fisheries Commission was established; it meets twice a year to discuss matters of mutual concern such as fish conservation. British and Argentine scientists co-operate on the transfer of data on fisheries between the two countries.

In November 1991 the Falklands Governor issued a proclamation providing for the Crown's rights over the seabed and subsoil of the Falkland Islands continental shelf. Legislation was also passed permitting seismic surveys in Falklands waters. Argentina, too, updated its legislation on maritime jurisdiction. British and Argentine representatives have discussed the scope for co-operation on these issues.

Government

Administration

The UN Charter contains important principles concerning the administration of dependent territories. The United Nations recognises Britain as the 'administering power' for the Islands. Article 73 imposes an obligation on Britain to treat the interests of the Islanders as paramount and to ensure their political, economic, social and educational advancement. In particular, Britain is obliged to develop self-government, to take due account of the political aspirations of the Islanders and to assist them in the progressive development of their free political institutions.

The present constitution came into force in October 1985. Its preamble says that all peoples have the right of self-determination and that every person in the Islands has the right to liberty, security, freedom of expression and conscience, and freedom of assembly and association.

Executive authority is exercised by the Governor who is appointed by the Queen. The Governor is advised by an Executive Council, consisting of three members of the Legislative Council, plus the Chief Executive and the Financial Secretary.

The Governor is President of the Legislative Council which has eight elected members; the other two members are the Chief Executive and the Financial Secretary. The ex-officio members do not have the right to vote in either council. The Legislative Council has the power to make laws for the territory and is concerned with the administration of the Islands, their general development, social services and education. Members can introduce a bill or propose a motion, legislation being passed by a simple majority.

Stanley's population elects four Legislative Council members, the other four coming from the rest of the Islands, known as the 'Camp' (from the Spanish 'campo' for field). There is universal adult suffrage and the voting age is 18 and above.

The Commander British Forces is responsible for defence and internal security, with the exception of the police.

The Judiciary

The judicial and legal system consists of a Supreme Court, a Magistrates' Court presided over by the senior magistrate, and a court of summary jurisdiction presided over by a bench of two or more magistrates. The Court of Appeal hears appeals from the Supreme Court. In some cases there is a final appeal to the Judicial Committee of the Privy Council. The Court of Appeal and the Judicial Committee sit in London. There is a resident Attorney General.

Defence

The Islands are defended by a British garrison maintained at the minimum size required to ensure their security and prevent a repetition of the events of 1982. The airport at Mount Pleasant has permitted some reduction in forces stationed on the Islands. The garrison is commanded by the Commander British Forces, who is responsible for all military matters.

The Economy

The economy is small and relatively undiversified. There are few natural resources, the population is small and the Islands are remote from external markets. Almost all the land is covered with natural pasture of low nutritional value and is devoted mainly to sheep ranching for the production of wool, which has been the traditional mainstay of the economy and the principal domestic export.

The development of the Islands was closely linked with the Falkland Islands Company, founded in 1851, which was the largest landowner and trading company until, in April 1991, it sold its remaining four farms to the Falkland Islands Government. Only about 4 per cent of the land area is now owned by overseas interests. The Falkland Islands Company has become a trading company with interests in construction and services to the fishing industry.

There are few areas of introduced pasture, and arable agriculture is limited to a small acreage of oats grown from hay. Most householders grow their own vegetables.

There are no proven minerals, although some offshore areas within territorial waters show some potential for hydrocarbon deposits; seismic surveys of promising offshore areas were carried out in early 1993. No definite details of the presence of hydrocarbons will be available for some years. In recent years the Islands have derived most of their revenue from the sale of fishing licences.

Development

In 1975 the British Government commissioned an economic study by Lord Shackleton to determine the prospects for the development and diversification of the economy and the best means of achieving this. Published in 1976, Lord Shackleton's report recommended the establishment of a tourism industry, agricultural and land reform, the enlargement of the airport and the development of a fishing industry, and offshore oil and gas production.

The construction of an airport at Stanley, which opened in 1979, was one of a number of infrastructure projects supported by British development assistance between 1977 and 1981. Other projects included improvements to electricity supplies, roads, internal air services, public works and education. In addition, professional expertise and advice was made available by Britain.

Following the 1982 conflict, Lord Shackleton's team was asked to bring its 1976 recommendations up to date. Many of the recommendations of the new report were accepted by the British Government, which in 1982 announced the provision of £31 million over six years for the development of the Islands' economy. The development programme was managed by the Falkland Islands Government and by the Falkland Islands Development Corporation (FIDC). The FIDC allocates loans and grants to new enterprises and takes up shares in enterprises and services. It has a wide remit to encourage and assist economic development and to advise the Falkland Islands Government. The main objectives of the Corporation are to:

—provide planning, advisory and financial assistance to local business enterprises;

—restrict development projects to locally manageable proportions and, whenever possible, build on existing resources;

—maximise export potential and encourage import substitution;

Knitwear being produced from Falklands wool at Port Howard.

Growing lettuces at the hydroponic farm at Stanley.

An 'Islander' aircraft touches down on a grass airstrip on Sea Lion Island, south of East Falkland.

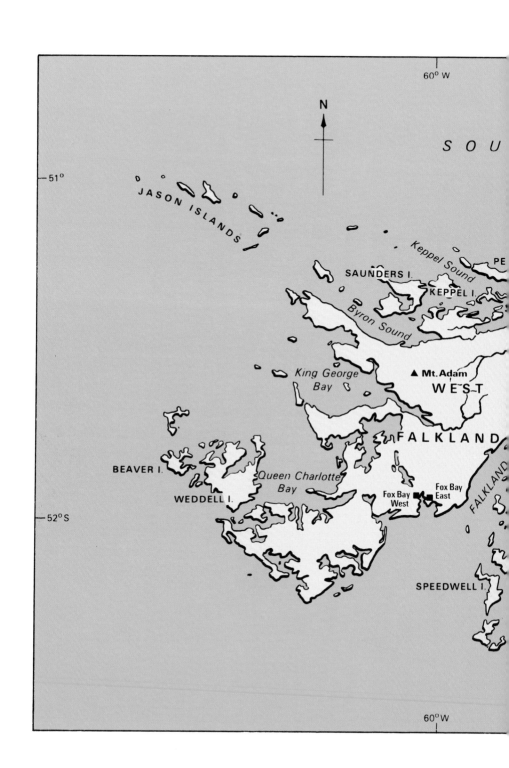

ATLANTIC

CEAN

North Falkland
Sound

Foul
Bay

Douglas

Port San Carlos

Teal Inlet

EAST

Grantham
Sound

Mt. Usborne

Darwin

Goose Green

ALKLAND

LAFONIA

Adventure
Sound

Low
Bay

Lively
Sound

Bay of
Harbours

Port Louis

Green
Patch

Berkeley Sound

Mt. Kent

STANLEY

Fitzroy

Mount Pleasant
Airport

Choiseul Sound

LIVELY I.

52° S

| 0 | 10 | 20 | 30 | 40 | 50 MILES |
| 0 | | 20 | 40 | | 60 KILOMETRES |

58°

The Falkland Islands are renowned for their wildlife.

A visitor photographs rare king penguins.

A female
elephant seal
on Sea Lion
Island.

—provide a high level of training;

—maximise the use of outside investment in conjunction with local resources;

—encourage owner/management of all enterprises and provide incentives to achieve this; and

—seek immigrants to undertake projects where there is a proven need but no suitable local expertise.

Set up in 1984, the FIDC operated with aid funding from Britain's Overseas Development Administration during the first eight years of its operation. Since July 1992 it has been financed by the Falkland Islands Government.

Fisheries

The bulk of government revenue comes from fisheries, following the introduction in February 1987 of the 150-mile Falkland Islands Interim Conservation and Management Zone (FICZ). Commercial fishing in the south-west Atlantic began in the early 1970s but did not have much impact on the Islands until the creation of the Zone. The Zone was introduced to meet concern about the increased levels of uncontrolled fishing close to the Falklands. All fishing within the Zone is licensed by the Falkland Islands Government and is determined by conservation and management imperatives. Revenue from the sale of fishing licences was about £26 million in 1991–92.

The main resources in the fishery are illex squid which are fished by squid jigging vessels from the Far East and loligo squid which are taken by trawlers from a number of European countries. Other species fished include blue whiting, hake and hoki. The illex squid have an annual life cycle; within one year, they hatch, feed and grow, migrate south from 45° into the FICZ, and then migrate northwards again to spawn and die. In order to give them greater protection from uncontrolled fishing when migrating, the 150-mile FICZ was reinforced in November 1990 by an Outer Conservation Zone some 322 km (200 miles) from coastal baselines.

The fishery provides commercial opportunities for Falklands companies to provide support services to the fishing fleets and to become involved in fishing. The Government Fishery Department administers the fishery and the management system designed to ensure the survival of the illex squid species.

In order to ensure that conservation targets are reached, the number of licensed vessels is limited and catch data are collected each day to monitor stocks. The fishing zone is policed by two fisheries patrol vessels and two patrol aircraft.

Agriculture

The main achievement in agriculture has been the land reform programme. In 1980 some 76 per cent of the land area was owned by absentee landlords and the land consisted of 36 large farms. Reinvestment was minimal, employment was decreasing and the industry was in general decline. Following Lord Shackleton's recommendations contained in reports published in 1976 and 1982, land ownership has changed completely through a programme of purchase and subdivision allied to a scheme of capital grants for reinvestment.

In 1991 the Falkland Islands Government purchased the four remaining farms owned by the Falkland Islands Company; these farms equalled 25 per cent of the total farm land of the Islands. By 1991 there were over 90 owner-occupied farms. The average farm size is 33,416 acres. Some 2,000 tons of wool are produced from the 650,000 sheep.

The Agricultural Department is responsible for veterinary services and for applying ordinances designed to prevent the importation and spread of plant and animal diseases. The Department's scientific research helps farmers introduce improved farming systems. In 1991 the Falkland Islands Government invested some £250,000 to purchase a national sheep stud flock from Australia in order to improve the quality of Falklands wool.

There is an agricultural co-operative—Falkland Farmers—which provides basic agricultural supplies to farmers at a reasonable price. A dairy complex provides Stanley residents with fresh milk and some other dairy products. There is also a dairy at Port Howard on West Falkland. A hydroponic market garden grows salad crops using the nutrient film technique. Produce is purchased by Islanders as well as by fishing fleets and the Ministry of Defence.

An experimental herd of cashmere goats has been imported to test their suitability to Falklands conditions.

Industries and Services

The FIDC has helped establish businesses in construction, manufacturing, food production, retailing and services such as accountancy. A spinning mill was set up at Fox Bay on West Falkland to add value to Falklands wool through the production of machine and hand knitting yarns and finished garments.

An area in Stanley has been subdivided into 50 sites which are being rented or sold to private businesses.

Tourism

Through its subsidiary, the Falkland Islands Tourist Board, the FIDC has created the necessary infrastructure for tourism. There are tourist lodges at the four main wildlife and activity centres—

Pebble Island, Port Howard, San Carlos and Sea Lion Island. In other settlements and in Stanley accommodation is in two modern hotels and in small family-run hotels or guest houses.

The Tourist Board co-operates with a number of specialist British and European tour operators who feature Falklands holidays in their brochures. About 5,000 cruise ship clients and land-based tourists visited the Islands in the 1991–92 summer.

The Islands are a haven for bird watchers, wildlife enthusiasts and photographers. Millions of seabirds nest on the Islands, including five species of penguin and the black-browed albatross. Mammals include sea lions and elephant seals. Angling holidays have extended the tourist season since migratory sea trout are present in Falklands waters during the autumn and the spring. A permanent fishing camp on the San Carlos River was completed in 1993.

Labour

About one-third of the labour force is employed in sheep farming. In Stanley the main sources of employment are government and public services, trading and shipping. There are two trade unions—the Falkland Islands General Employees Union and the Civil Servants Association. The former is a general union and is affiliated to the International Confederation of Free Trade Unions. The other union represents the interests of government white-collar workers.

Legislation is in force which regulates minimum wages, working conditions and compensation for accidents at work; there is also an arbitration procedure in the event of a labour dispute which cannot be settled by direct negotiations.

In cases where job vacancies cannot be filled from local resources, skilled technical and professional personnel are recruited on contract terms from Britain by the Falkland Islands Government. There is virtually no unemployment.

Trade

Exports consist almost entirely of wool, hides and skins. Most food items, fuels, manufactured goods and machinery are imported. External trade is almost exclusively with Britain, although efforts are being made to increase commercial contacts with Chile and Uruguay.

Taxation

People pay income tax at 20 per cent on the first £20,000 of chargeable income; this goes up to 25 per cent on the remainder of chargeable income. This takes effect after deduction of various personal allowances.

Companies have to pay tax on income after deduction of allowable expenditure and depreciation allowances at 25 per cent on all profits, whether distributed or not. A further 10 per cent is payable on any part of the company's profits which it pays to a person not ordinarily resident in the Islands; this also applies to payments made to a company not resident in the Islands.

There is a double taxation agreement with Britain.

Social Welfare

Education

Education is free and compulsory for all children between the ages of 5 and 15, and children who may benefit from further education are encouraged to continue their studies until they are 16. The Government provides equipment and supplies to education throughout the Islands and operates several schools in the larger settlements.

There are two schools in Stanley, which use British teaching methods and examination systems. The primary school has 12 members of staff and 170 pupils of 5–11 years. The senior school has 14 specialist teachers and 135 pupils. Many teachers come from Britain or New Zealand and local teachers are trained in Britain.

In 1992 a new community school was opened. This provides modern facilities for science, technical and language studies while providing ample space for current demands and future growth. It has up-to-date sporting facilities and is connected to a new 25-metre swimming pool. The community school is also designed to play a major part in adult education; it contains a public library which offers a postal service to Camp residents.

The community school offers 16 subject courses for the General Certificate of Secondary Education, including English language, English literature, history, geography, various science subjects, design and technology, art and Spanish. School leavers take with them a record of achievement outlining the attainments secured during their time at school.

Suitable students are financed to attend the Peter Symonds Sixth Form College in Winchester for two years and after that to university or technical college if these are appropriate. There are also opportunities for young people to take vocational courses in Britain. Students' return passage to the Islands for holidays comes from public funds. In 1991 some 30 students received training in British schools and colleges.

In the rural areas younger children attend small settlement schools or are visited by one of a team of six travelling teachers for two out of every seven weeks. Settlement teachers receive support from the Camp Education Unit which also sets work for children to do between travelling teachers' visits. The Unit also conducts daily radio lessons, through a VHF network.

Most of the older Camp children attend school in Stanley and live in a boarding hostel which has purpose-built dormitories and accommodation for dining, study and recreation.

Health

The Health Department is responsible for preventive and curative medical services in the territory. A board of health deals with public health problems as they arise. The Chief Medical Officer, who sits on the board, is responsible for advising the Falkland Islands Government on health policy.

The Islands' only civilian hospital, the King Edward VII Memorial Hospital, was rebuilt in 1987 following a fire in 1984 and is located in Stanley. It offers modern facilities, has a full complement of 87 medical, dental and nursing staff, and is shared between the civilian and the military authorities. Medical services are run from the hospital, including a general practitioner service for

Stanley and routine and emergency flying doctor services for farm settlements.

Specialist advice and assistance is given by the Royal Army Medical Corps, and the Royal Air Force provides an aeromedical evacuation service to Britain for the seriously ill.

There is no private system of medical care. Medical and dental treatment and drugs are provided free to residents but all employers are required to pay a medical services levy at the rate of 2.5 per cent of gross wages/salaries paid to employees; of this, 1 per cent is paid by the employee and 1.5 per cent by the employer.

Social Security

There is a system of family allowances and two retirement pension schemes, one contributory and the other non-contributory, which cover all people reaching the age of 64.

Communications and Services

Transport

A programme of rural road building is under way. There is an unsurfaced road linking Stanley with Port Louis and Teal Inlet. Another road goes to Mount Pleasant and has recently been extended to Darwin and Goose Green. Under construction is a road linking Port Howard with Fox Bay. Travel elsewhere in the countryside is by four-wheel drive vehicle, motorbike or horse. Unsurfaced tracks connect most settlements in the countryside. Roads in Stanley are nearly all fully paved.

Internal air transport is provided by the Falkland Islands Government Air Service which operates three nine-seater Britten-Norman 'Islander' aircraft. There are some 40 grass and beach airstrips serving almost every settlement in the Islands.

Freight is normally transported around the Islands by small coastal vessels. A new ship, the *Tamar*, was delivered in 1993 and is designed to carry fuel and other supplies to farms and outlying islands and to collect wool for onward shipment to Britain by quarterly charter vessel.

There are two flights a week to the Islands from RAF Brize Norton in Oxfordshire to Mount Pleasant International Airport. The journey takes about 18 hours in a Tristar aircraft with a short refuelling stop on Ascension Island. Flights on this service can be arranged through the Falkland Islands Government Office in London. Medium-haul flights are taken by Stanley airport.

An air service operating out of Punta Arenas in southern Chile with a 17-seater aircraft makes weekly flights to and from the Islands during the summer months; in the winter months the service is fortnightly.

There is a six-weekly shipping service between Britain and the Islands. Surface links with South America are provided by the *Tamar* and by a Chilean vessel, which offer monthly services between the southern Chilean port of Punta Arenas and Stanley.

Communications

Air mail is received and dispatched twice a week and surface mail once every five weeks.

External telecommunications are provided by Cable and Wireless plc, which operates a world-wide service. A £5.5 million telecommunications network covering the Islands has been installed recently. This provides international direct dialling facilities, together with telex, facsimile and high-speed data services.

Media

In addition to the official Gazette, two weekly newspapers are published. The Falkland Islands Broadcasting Station broadcasts 24 hours a day and also uses programmes from the British Forces Broadcasting Service. The BBC World Service English programmes are also received in the Islands.

There is one television channel, which is operated by the British Forces and which transmits programmes supplied by British television companies. The system has operated at Mount Pleasant and in Stanley for several years and is being extended throughout the rest of the Islands. Videos are in widespread use and there are several well-stocked commercial video libraries.

Public Utilities

The government-owned electricity power station, opened in 1973 and extended in 1985 to a capacity of 6.3 MW, supplies power to Stanley via a new distribution system. There is a smaller station at Fox Bay East on West Falkland. Most farms and settlements have their own private generating plants. The FIDC is supporting schemes to make the Islands more self-sufficient in energy production. It has also assisted the installation of wind generators at Pebble Island and is supporting a hydro-electric power scheme. Solar power is also increasingly used for outlying farms.

Clean water is supplied to the population in Stanley by a water purification and filtration plant. The sewerage system has been improved recently.

South Georgia and the South Sandwich Islands

South Georgia

South Georgia lies 1,290 km (800 miles) east-south-east of the Falkland Islands, and the South Sandwich Islands some 760 km (460 miles) south-east of South Georgia. The population of South Georgia comprises the staff of a small scientific station at Bird Island, staffed by the British Antarctic Survey, and a detachment of troops stationed at King Edward Point. All food is imported and there are no exports. The South Sandwich Islands have no inhabitants.

The constitution for the dependency was promulgated in 1985. The Governor of the Falkland Islands is also the Commissioner for South Georgia and the South Sandwich Islands; in this capacity he consults the Falklands Executive Council on those matters relating to the territory which might affect the Falkland Islands.

South Georgia has an area of 3,755 sq km (1,450 sq miles) and is some 160 km (100 miles) long, with a minimum breadth of 32 km (20 miles). The land is very mountainous, rising to 2,933 m (9,625 ft), the valleys being filled with glaciers, many of which descend to the sea. The climate is very severe, the mountains being largely ice- and snow-covered throughout the year. The only indigenous mammals are seals, but there are two thriving herds of wild reindeer, which were first introduced in 1911.

South Sandwich Islands

The South Sandwich Islands consist of a chain of actively volcanic islands some 240 km (150 miles) long. The climate is wholly Antarctic. In the late winter the islands may be surrounded by pack ice. The prevalent western storms always make landing difficult.

History

South Georgia was sighted at least twice between 1675 and 1756, but the first landing was that of Captain James Cook in 1775. The South Sandwich Islands were discovered during the same voyage. Thereafter, South Georgia was much visited by sealers of many nationalities, who reaped a rich harvest from the immense number of fur seals and elephant seals which frequented these shores. By 1815, the seal slaughter had reached such proportions that the sealers were beginning to look elsewhere.

The British Government annexed South Georgia and the South Sandwich Islands by letters patent in 1908. Since then the Islands have been under continuous British administration, apart from the short period of illegal Argentine occupation in 1982. Whaling began in the twentieth century and expanded in the period up to 1918. South Georgia was the most important centre and six shore factories were established. After the second world war three shore stations were worked but all ceased operating by the end of 1965.

Since 1965 the main economic activity in the territory has been fishing by distant water fishing fleets. The territory's income is derived from fees from fishing vessels transhipping their catches in the sheltered bays of South Georgia and from the sale of postage stamps and proceeds from tourism.

Argentina also claims South Georgia and the South Sandwich Islands, but Britain rejects these claims as being without legal or historical justification. During the 1982 conflict Britain repossessed both sets of Islands from Argentina, following their illegal occupation.

Appendix: The 1982 Crisis

British–Argentine Talks

The Argentine claim to the Falkland Islands was emphasised again in January 1982, when the Buenos Aires Government sent a communication to the British Government stating that British recognition of Argentine sovereignty over the Islands remained the main requirement for a solution to the dispute. It called for negotiations which would culminate in recognition of Argentine sovereignty. Argentina proposed the establishment of a permanent negotiating commission which would last for one year.

In response, the British Government reaffirmed that it was in no doubt about British sovereignty and that it could not accept that the purpose of the negotiations was eventual British recognition of Argentine sovereignty. It was, however, ready to continue the negotiating process in order to find an early and peaceful solution to the dispute which could be accepted by both governments and the Islanders.

Discussion between the two governments took place at the end of February 1982 in New York, the Argentines pressing for the establishment of the commission within a month with a view to holding a first meeting at the beginning of April. It was agreed that the commission would be set up with a working life of one year and that its work would be conducted without prejudice to the sovereignty position of either government. The joint communiqué issued at the end of the meeting on 1 March said: 'The meeting took place in a cordial and positive spirit. The two sides reaffirmed their resolve to find a solution to the sovereignty dispute and considered in detail an Argentine proposal for procedures to make better progress in this sense. They agreed to inform their governments accordingly.'

On the day that the joint communiqué was issued, the Argentine Ministry of Foreign Affairs issued a unilateral communiqué saying that the commission had to speed up the negotiations to achieve recognition of Argentine sovereignty. If an early solution to the dispute did not occur, Argentina reserved the right to 'terminate the working of this mechanism and to choose freely the procedure which best accords with her interests'.

Commenting on the outcome of the New York talks, Britain's negotiator, Richard Luce, told the House of Commons on 3 March that he had made it clear that 'we had no doubts about British sovereignty, and that no solution could be agreed that was not acceptable to the Islanders and to the House. . . . '

Events Leading to the Argentine Invasion

In March the British Government stated that the negotiating commission should encompass all aspects of possible approaches to a solution of the dispute without prejudice to either side's view on sovereignty and that the negotiations could not be pursued against a background of threats from either side of retaliatory action if they broke down.

Relations between Britain and Argentina deteriorated later in the month, when a large group of Argentine workmen, sent on a commercial contract to dismantle a disused whaling station, landed in the British territory of South Georgia on 19 March without seeking authorisation from the British authorities. They had been told in advance of the need to comply with normal immigration procedures in South Georgia by first seeking permission to land. This was ignored and the party hoisted the Argentine flag. Although the Argentine ship later departed, a dozen or so men remained; the British Government told the Argentine Government that it regarded these men as being on British territory illegally and requested co-operation in arranging for their departure while pointing out that the position could be regularised if they were to seek proper authorisation. A British naval ice-patrol vessel, HMS *Endurance,* was ordered to the area.

On 25 March an Argentine Antarctic supply ship made further deliveries to the men. The Argentine Foreign Minister asserted that the men in South Georgia were on Argentine territory and would be given full protection. Two days later, restating its claim to the Falkland Islands, South Georgia and the South Sandwich Islands, Argentina rejected Britain's proposal to regularise the situation.

In a further endeavour to reach a peaceful settlement, the British Government proposed on 31 March that a special envoy should be sent to Buenos Aires for discussions. On the same day Britain received information that a large Argentine fleet was heading for the Falkland Islands. That evening the then Prime Minister, Margaret Thatcher, contacted US President Ronald Reagan, requesting him to intervene directly with the Argentine Government and promising that Britain would take no action to escalate the dispute.

On 1 April Argentina said that it was pointless to send an envoy to discuss the South Georgia incident. It would, however, have been prepared to accept the dispatch of a British representative to negotiate the transfer of sovereignty over the Falkland

Islands. On the same day President Reagan urged restraint on the Argentine Government and the then UN Secretary-General, Perez de Cuellar, met the Argentine and British UN Permanent Representatives asking them to refrain from the use of force.

During the afternoon of 1 April Britain called for an emergency meeting of the UN Security Council. At the Council meeting, held that evening, the British Permanent Representative, Sir Anthony Parsons, pointed out that there was strong evidence that an Argentine invasion of the Islands would take place on 2 April. He therefore requested the Council to call on Argentina to refrain from the use of force.

Sir Anthony also assured the Council that the British Government had conducted the recent negotiations in perfect good faith and that it was ready to continue these in the future. 'What is unacceptable is an attempt to change the situation by force.' The Argentine representative claimed that there was a British threat to use force against Argentina's territory, leaving it no alternative but to adopt the necessary measures to ensure its self-defence. Argentina was ready to negotiate provided Britain made a prior recognition of Argentine sovereignty over the Islands.

The President of the Council read out a statement on its behalf calling on Argentina and Britain not to resort to force and instead to continue the search for a diplomatic solution. Sir Anthony said that the British Government would comply with the Council's call and continue the search for a diplomatic solution.

Argentine Invasion

On 2 April Argentine forces occupied the Islands. In response, the Security Council met on the same day following another British request. Sir Anthony described the Argentine action as a 'wanton act of armed force' and a 'blatant violation of the United Nations Charter'. The mandatory Security Council Resolution 502 was passed, demanding an immediate cessation of hostilities and an immediate withdrawal of Argentine forces from the Islands. It also called upon both governments 'to seek a diplomatic solution to their differences and to respect fully the purposes and principles of the Charter of the United Nations'. Argentina, however, refused to comply.

European Community foreign ministers also issued a declaration condemning Argentina and appealing for a withdrawal of its forces.

Britain's Response

Although a British naval task force was sent to the South Atlantic in response to the Argentine invasion, the time taken for it to arrive allowed an opportunity to solve the problem by peaceful means. The British Government made it clear that it was ready to use force to repossess the Islands if such efforts were to fail.

Britain also sought to influence Argentina through economic and diplomatic pressure. In addition to severing diplomatic relations, the Government froze all Argentine financial assets held in Britain, banned imports from Argentina, suspended new export credit cover and banned the export to Argentina of arms and other military equipment. On 10 April European Community foreign ministers announced an embargo on arms and military equipment for Argentina and on 16 April banned imports from Argentina.

At a special meeting of the North Atlantic Council of the North Atlantic Treaty Organisation (NATO), held on 2 April, member states expressed deep concern about the dispute and requested both parties to refrain from the threat or use of force. Britain's NATO allies subsequently condemned the Argentine use of force.

The Search for a Negotiated Solution

Although the British Government emphasised the need for total Argentine withdrawal from the Islands in line with Resolution 502, it was prepared to discuss possible arrangements for supervising the withdrawal and for a degree of international involvement in the administration of the Islands. At the same time it remained committed to certain principles, notably the need to uphold international law through the implementation of Resolution 502 and freedom for the Falkland Islanders to participate, through their elected representatives, in the running of their own affairs and to express their wishes about the Islands' future.

In addition, while ready to enter negotiations for a long-term settlement of the dispute, the Government stated that it was only prepared to do so on condition that there was no attempt to predetermine or prejudge the outcome, whether on sovereignty or other matters.

United States Initiative

The first diplomatic effort to secure an interim settlement, based on Resolution 502, was made by the US Secretary of State, Alexander Haig, with the full support of the British Government. Mr Haig had talks with both countries and put forward a set of compromise proposals. These involved:

— the withdrawal of Argentine and British forces;

— the ending of economic sanctions;

— the establishment of a British–United States–Argentine interim authority for the Islands;

—Argentine participation in the Islands' local administration;

—procedures for encouraging co-operation in the development of the Islands; and

—a framework for final negotiations on a final settlement taking account of British and Argentine interests and the wishes of the Islanders.

Although these proposals presented certain difficulties, Britain expressed willingness to consider them. The Argentine junta rejected them by demanding an immediate assurance of eventual sovereignty or an immediate de facto role in governing the Islands which would lead to sovereignty.

Following the Argentine refusal to compromise, President Reagan ordered the suspension of all military exports to Argentina and other economic sanctions on 30 April.

New Peace Proposals
Further discussions took place on a peace plan advanced by the Peruvian President and modified after discussions with Mr Haig. On 6 May the British Government accepted the idea of interim arrangements which provided for:

—a complete and supervised withdrawal of Argentine forces from the Islands matched by corresponding withdrawal of British forces;

—an immediate ceasefire following Argentine agreement to withdraw; and

—the appointment of a small group of countries acceptable to both sides who would supervise withdrawal, undertake the interim administration in consultation with the Islanders' elected representatives and assist in negotiating a definite agreement on the status of the Islands without prejudice to Britain's own principles or the wishes of the Islanders.

These proposals, which did not prejudge the shape of a final settlement, were rejected by the Argentine junta, which continued to insist that a transfer of sovereignty should be the precondition of negotiations.

UN Secretary-General's Initiative

The next attempt to achieve a peaceful settlement was undertaken by the UN Secretary-General, Perez de Cuellar. On 2 May he presented a number of proposals to both sides. Intended to be without prejudice to the rights, claims or positions of either party, the proposals included:

—the withdrawal by an agreed date of Argentine troops from the Islands and of British forces from the area around the Falkland Islands;

—negotiations by both governments to seek a diplomatic solution to their differences by an agreed date;

—the ending of hostilities and of economic sanctions; and

—transitional arrangements under which these measures would be supervised.

On 6 May Britain replied, stating that Resolution 502 had to be implemented without delay and that a ceasefire had to be unambiguously linked to the beginning of Argentine withdrawal within a fixed number of days.

Britain's Final Proposals

On 17 May Britain presented its final proposals to the UN Secretary-General in the form of a draft interim agreement between the British and Argentine Governments. This stated that

no provision of the interim agreement would 'in any way prejudice the rights, claims and positions of either party in the ultimate peaceful settlement of their dispute over the Islands'. The draft agreement provided for:

—complete Argentine withdrawal from the Islands within 14 days;

—a withdrawal of all British and Argentine armed forces to at least 150 nautical miles radius from the Islands (also within 14 days);

—international verification of the withdrawals;

—the lifting of exclusion zones; and

—the lifting of economic measures taken against Argentina.

In addition, the draft proposed that a UN Administrator, acceptable to Britain and Argentina, should be appointed by the Secretary-General to administer the government of the Islands in conformity with traditional laws and practices and in consultation with the Falklands Legislative and Executive Councils. The Administrator would also verify the withdrawal of all armed forces from the Islands and devise an effective method of ensuring their non-reintroduction.

The draft interim agreement also proposed that both parties should 'undertake to enter into negotiations in good faith under the auspices of the Secretary-General of the United Nations for the peaceful settlement of their dispute and to seek, with a sense of urgency, the completion of these negotiations by 31 December 1982'. The draft added: 'These negotiations shall be initiated without prejudice to the rights, claims or positions of the parties and without prejudgment of the outcome.'

The draft interim agreement was given to the UN Secretary-General, Sir Anthony Parsons making it clear that this was the furthest that Britain could go in the negotiations.

Replying on 19 May, Argentina wanted the withdrawal of forces to be completed in 30 days, followed by their return to their normal bases and areas of operation. The administration of the Islands was to be the exclusive responsibility of the United Nations (though with Argentine and British observers present). Argentina also wanted free access for its nationals to the Islands with respect to residence, work and property, and opposed the British view that the UN Administrator should exercise his powers in conformity with the laws and practices traditionally observed in the Islands.

As for negotiations concerning the Islands' future, Argentina stated that these should be initiated without prejudice to the rights, claims and positions of the two parties but would not accept an additional phrase stating that the outcome should not be pre-judged. Argentina also resisted a provision in the British draft designed to ensure that the interim arrangements should remain in place until a definitive agreement about the future of the Islands could be implemented.

Britain was unable to accept Argentina's response because it included unbalanced provisions regarding withdrawal. Had both sides returned their forces to their normal bases, Argentina's would have been 640 km (400 miles) away from the Islands and the British 12,900 km (8,000 miles) away with nothing to prevent the return of Argentine troops. Equally unsatisfactory features of the Argentine response were the destruction of the previous democratic structures of government on the Islands, opportunities for Argentina to change the character of the Islands in its favour by flooding them with Argentine nationals, and terms of reference for long-term negotiations which led in only one direction.

Following Argentina's rejection of the British draft interim agreement, the British Government withdrew these proposals.

On 21 May the UN Secretary-General reported to the Security Council on his attempts to broker a peaceful settlement. In response, Sir Anthony Parsons said that Argentina had in practice rejected Resolution 502 by reinforcing its forces on the Islands and imposing its military government in place of democratic rule. In these circumstances Britain had no choice but to exercise its right of self-defence under Article 51 of the Charter.

Further Efforts
On 26 May the Security Council unanimously reaffirmed Resolution 502, requested the Secretary-General to undertake a renewed mission of good offices and urged both parties to co-operate fully with a view to ending the hostilities in and around the Islands.

The resolution asked the Secretary-General 'to enter into contact immediately with the parties with a view to negotiating mutually acceptable terms for a ceasefire, including, if necessary, arrangements for the dispatch of United Nations observers to monitor compliance with the terms of the ceasefire'. While supporting the resolution and promising full co-operation with the Secretary-General, Sir Anthony Parsons stressed that the only acceptable condition for a ceasefire was that it should be unequivocally linked with an immediate beginning of Argentine withdrawal.

On 2 June Sir Anthony told the Council that Britain would 'welcome a ceasefire which was inseparably linked to the commencement of the withdrawal of Argentine forces and to the completion of their withdrawal within a fixed period'. He made it plain that a ceasefire not linked to an Argentine withdrawal was inconsistent with Resolution 502 and that the call for an unconditional ceasefire would leave Argentine forces in position.

On 4 June the Security Council voted on a draft resolution requesting both parties to observe a ceasefire and to initiate, simultaneously with the ceasefire, the implementation of Resolutions 502 and 505 in their entirety. Britain and the United States voted against the resolution on the grounds that it did not meet the criteria of an immediate ceasefire linked inseparably to the immediate and total withdrawal of Argentine forces from the Falkland Islands.

Military Developments

From the outset Britain made it clear that, while committed to a diplomatic solution, it would be prepared, if necessary, to use force to secure the withdrawal of the occupying troops, in accordance with Article 51 of the UN Charter.

The British naval task force set sail in early April and comprised aircraft carriers, guided missile destroyers, frigates, assault ships with landing craft, and supporting vessels. Also embarked were a strong force of Royal Marine Commandos, Sea Harrier aircraft and many anti-submarine and troop-carrying helicopters. Ships from the Merchant Navy were requisitioned to carry troops and supplies. More than a hundred Royal Navy and other ships were involved in the operation and over 28,000 servicemen and civilians, men and women, sailed with the task force.

After the dispatch of the task force, the Defence Secretary, John Nott, told the House of Commons on 7 April that a maritime exclusion zone would be established around the Islands in order to deny the Argentine forces means of reinforcement and re-supply from the mainland. On 12 April the zone came into force, the outer limit being a circle of 200 nautical miles radius from the centre of the Islands.

Britain pointed out that any Argentine warships or naval auxiliaries found within the zone would be treated as hostile and liable to be attacked by British forces. At the same time it made clear that this measure was without prejudice to Britain's right to take whatever additional measures might be needed in exercise of the right to self-defence. On 23 April the British Government informed Argentina that 'any approach on the part of Argentine warships, including submarines, naval auxiliaries or military aircraft which could amount to a threat to interfere with the mission of the British forces in the South Atlantic will encounter the appropriate response'.

Following the arrival of the task force in the area of the Falkland Islands, Britain announced that the maritime exclusion zone would become a total exclusion zone with effect from 30 April and would be applicable to all ships and aircraft, whether military or civil, operating in support of Argentina's illegal occupation. On 7 May Argentina was told that any of its warships or military aircraft more than 12 nautical miles from the Argentine coast would be treated as hostile and dealt with as appropriate. This move was, in the British Government's view, necessary because of the proximity of Argentine bases, the threat posed by Argentine carrier-borne aircraft and the ability of hostile forces to approach undetected in bad weather and at low level.

South Georgia Landing

On 25 April British troops, supported by a number of warships, landed on South Georgia and quickly secured the surrender of the Argentine forces at Grytviken. During the first phase of the operation the Argentine submarine *Santa Fe* was attacked and disabled. On 26 April the Argentine commander formally surrendered. No lives were lost on either side during the operation.

Aerial and Naval Engagements

A series of aerial and naval engagements took place before British forces landed on the Islands. On 23 April the Argentine cruiser *General Belgrano* was torpedoed by a British submarine on the grounds that it represented a threat to British forces. The British warship HMS *Sheffield* was attacked by Argentine-launched Exocet missiles and caught fire, the crew having to abandon ship; nearly 20 men on board were killed.

Periodic bombardments of Argentine military installations on the Islands continued as the British blockade tightened its grip.

British Landing

On 21 May, following the final breakdown in negotiations, a major amphibious landing began at 03.20 hours local time in the area of San Carlos in East Falkland. Artillery and air defence weapons were successfully landed, followed by all the infantry units.

At 10.30 hours a series of Argentine air attacks was made on British vessels, 17 combat aircraft being lost. Five British ships were damaged, including the frigate HMS *Ardent* which was sunk; 22 crew members were killed.

Although British forces consolidated their positions on 22 May, there were renewed Argentine air attacks which severely damaged the frigate HMS *Antelope*. An unexploded bomb remained on board, but despite efforts to defuse it a large explosion took place and the ship sank, a bomb disposal officer losing his life.

In other Argentine air attacks in the South Atlantic, the destroyer HMS *Coventry* was hit by several bombs on 25 May and later capsized, with the loss of about 20 lives. On the same day the Merchant Navy ship the *Atlantic Conveyor* was hit by an Exocet missile and was set on fire, 13 crew members being killed.

British forces advanced from the San Carlos bridgehead and, following a battle in which 16 British soldiers (including the commanding officer) and a much greater number of Argentine soldiers died, took the settlements of Goose Green and Darwin on 28 May. Over 900 prisoners were taken. In another and more northerly advance from the San Carlos bridgehead, other forces seized Douglas and Teal Inlet. By the beginning of June the high ground around Mount Kent, some 19 km (12 miles) from Stanley, had been occupied.

On 8 June some 50 British soldiers were killed when Argentine aircraft attacked two Royal Navy Fleet Auxiliary landing ships, the *Sir Galahad* and *Sir Tristram*, as they were about to land troops at Fitzroy. Further casualties occurred on 12 June when 13 crewmen were killed during an attack on HMS *Glamorgan*, which was providing naval support to land forces advancing on Stanley.

Following rapid advances to capture high ground dominating Stanley, Argentine defences were soon breached, and, following talks between the British and Argentine sides, the Argentine forces surrendered, including over 11,000 men. Under the terms of the surrender the Argentine soldiers handed over their weapons and ammunition and Britain undertook to treat them in accordance with conditions set out in the 1949 Geneva Convention. Argentine prisoners of war were later returned to Argentina on British ships, although some 600 remained in custody pending an official cessation of hostilities.

On 15 June Britain sent notes to Argentina through the Swiss and Brazilian embassies seeking confirmation of the total cessation of hostilities. In response Argentina stated on 18 June that this would be achieved only if certain conditions were fulfilled, including the withdrawal of British forces from the Islands. In a letter to the UN Security Council's President sent on 23 June, Sir Anthony Parsons said that this condition was totally unacceptable to Britain and that its forces were present to defend the Islands and their people against further attacks and to help the Islanders repair the extensive damage caused by the Argentine invasion and occupation. Sir Anthony emphasised that the Islands were British territory with a British population and that there could, therefore, be no question of withdrawing British forces.

On 9 July a British message was sent to the Argentine Government, via the Swiss Embassy in Buenos Aires, noting that there had been no further hostilities in the South Atlantic since 14 June and that the Argentine Foreign Minister had stated on 5 July that there was a *de facto* ceasefire on the part of Argentina. It therefore proposed that the remaining prisoners of war in British hands should be returned to Argentina. Two days later the Argentine Government replied saying that 'in view of the present state of *de facto* cessation of hostilities, arrangements should be made for the prisoners' return'. On 12 July Britain expressed satisfaction at Argentina's acceptance of the ending of active hostilities and said that the 600 prisoners would be returned.

Restoration of British Administration

On 25 June the former Governor returned to the Islands as Civil Commissioner with responsibility for all matters relating to civil administration. The commander of British land forces was designated Military Commissioner with responsibility for defence and internal security, excluding the police.

Further Reading

£

Battle for the Falklands (revised
edition). Max Hastings and Simon
Jenkins.
ISBN 0 7181 2578 9.   Michael Joseph   1992   25.00

Falklands: South Atlantic Islands.
Ian J. Strange.
ISBN 0 7090 2852 0.   Hale   1987   14.95

*Field Guide to the Wildlife of the
Falkland Islands and South Georgia.*
Ian J. Strange.
ISBN 0 00 219839 8.   Collins Reference   1992   14.99

Index

Printed in the UK for HMSO.
Dd.0296522, 6/93, C30, 51-2423, 5673

THE ANNUAL PICTURE

BRITAIN
1993

AN OFFICIAL HANDBOOK

BRITAIN HANDBOOK

The annual picture of Britain is provided by *Britain: An Official Handbook* - the forty-fourth edition will be published early in 1993. It is the unrivalled reference book about Britain, packed with information and statistics on every facet of British life.

With a circulation of over 20,000 worldwide, it is essential for libraries, educational institutions, business organisations and individuals needing easy access to reliable and up-to-date information, and is supported in this role by its sister publication, *Current Affairs: A Monthly Survey*.

Approx. 500 pages; 24 pages of colour illustrations; 16 maps; diagrams and tables throughout the text; and a statistical section. Price £19·50.

Buyers of Britain 1993: An Official Handbook *have the opportunity of a year's subscription to* Current Affairs *at 25 per cent off the published price of £35·80. They will also have the option of renewing their subscription next year at the same discount. Details in each copy of* Handbook, *from HMSO Publications Centre and at HMSO bookshops (see back of title page).*